S0-FQN-432

Desire

Sebastian Lopez

Washington, DC

2012

Copyright © 2012 by Sebastian Lopez

All rights reserved. No part of this publication may be reproduced, stored in a retrieval system, or transmitted, in any form or by any means, electronic, mechanical, photocopying, recording, or otherwise, without the prior written permission of the author.

To my teachers

Evgeny Mikhailovich Friedman

Patricia Carden

Savely Senderovich

There are more things in heaven and earth, Horatio,
than are dreamt of in your philosophy.

—Shakespeare

If you like piña coladas . . .

—Jimmy Buffett

Contents

Desire

Meiday Meiday

You can catch an ethereal tide
and rainbow
        above this tropical city
                and these lifeless skyscrapers . . .
        Come with me
I'm a boy,
        but I got a girly fun and wink . . .
Glide with me . . .
                It's like sparkled sweetest sex,
forbidden play and spirituality,
in a faraway sky,
        yet so close . . .

A Face

I know this girl. I can't see anything in her face, it's like a veil or a wall transparent that flows through the soft edge of the waterfall of nothing. I want to speak. I wish into her lithe beauty, a renegade in winter. Her face brims. It could almost swirl and get me high. Her frail shoulders are pillars of a stronghold, of an apparent world of normalcy, a poignant beauty encapsulated in a timeless chamber coolly lit like a candle by an unknown. Or she's the blue metropolitan sanctum. It's like she's a reflection of some God in the distance. I can't find any traces of anything I know in her countenance. She's stranger. So apparently normal and calm, stranger than any strange and beautiful person or song I've known. Her face is an ocean of normalcy, it is a frozen wind without context where nothing, no clothes or stockings or anything whatsoever, wants to fit. Her face radiates the beginning of nothing. It's like a crystal staircase into the flowering of a universal cloud. The face is a flowing into a pulsing state that is nowhere and nothing I know . . .

Drills

It's like making love to Marilyn Monroe
in nocturnal swimming pools
of tastelessly decorated American hotels.
"They're all these filthy people of good taste."
It's the sun beating down on a face,
its rays—these soft melodic pulsings—little exclamations
hitting the atmosphere of our bodies, of our faces . . .
Rain down on us.
Come in these tides of this playful God,
like jet planes.
I didn't know you
were human . . . like leaves of grass
in their resplendent vanity—
come into their release.
Like kind astronauts'
clear and careful warnings.

Mushroom

I was more like the plants. A feminine, slender,
naked body, beaming in white sunlight. Shiny
in the morning garden of a bemushroomed eternity.
White-vinyl helmeted, with ever prudent sight . . .
dabbling in the air . . .
waking . . . walking . . . suffering . . .
in slow and miniature movements,
in little awakenings. Shielded by the mushroom
mind like a bubble of psycho rain
from the eyes of the uninitiated in this place—
into this otherly holy mystery. Moving over a street
in a tropical city. Bemusement . . . a pleasant pining away . . .
Ever learning . . . nourishment . . . as I imbibe the moist
and etheric, beauteous and tender
and scientifically tiny lessons
of an unknown and tremendously
mysterious Logos
estranged by our society.

Moon

Our lives' tides and reasons hide behind their feminine appellations. In the small world the appellations form as these soft, lithe poses of raw female—dexterous and welded of fabled goddess. Fold these stories within. Build a black house behind the guise of today's and everyman's putrid emotive ships and impulses. Build the house behind the guises of yesterday's jaded songs that led to nowhere in particular. This is a house needed by your stinking heart and transfixing soul, by your unloved, unlathered mind—a mind wrought in beauty of desolation. A cold, white breeze ravishes through black bodies, lined up along a wall. This is the presence of your foremother's humility and dead-aired mystery. A moon-face appears, it oscillates between suns over languid bridge . . . This is the mother to weathers of freed dreams . . . Steal into work and revision with a wisp motor revving quietly above this little house on a stilt . . .

Come a cessation to all works and hives with this crystalline infiltration to peaks of miracle snow, caps of purity . . . Mother shrinks . . . The heart lightly despairs, broadcasts through oceans and skies to the ear of sweet sister and to her sewage of mimicry—knowing . . . Overlook the palaces of life with the carvings and sheddings of mother-pearled face—this serene, scattered, female moon. She's always one shedding shy of naught. She is shy of her paltry emptiness. A shy emptiness bears all like bones. Dark oceans follow her soft counsel—deafening, defeating her aptitude, her attitude. Barking dogs know not why they bark to her glistened speech . . . Don't ask them questions . . . A human motor gently revs. A turpentine ocean quietly flows like docile love and willow-swept pillow misery. A nice girl ponders through a window that is cracked open to the night. Rinse the night away. Rise, you freaks, in day's belonging. The abyssal of men, the workers and haulers, yield strongly and longly in such a fast and wide white tide. Yell through the magnifying glasses of peace. Yell through the petting of lassies. Her pages you'll never turn . . .

Green God

I want to know: do I get to throw my hands to the sky when I die? Do I get to throw my arms in the sky? And sigh? One last heave . . . One last rush . . .
Rushing me in . . . into your embrace . . .
We, barely bones, rattling on a verdant humming hill . . . sweet cadavers . . .
We are resonating to a melody,
Onerous,
owning us . . . and on . . . and on . . . A melody broken in little flutters,
Broken on our hands like the perfume of this place . . .
          Serenading this special, this so high and kind kindness
Overcome by this that is so infinite and wise . . .
That yields in these parts like candied rain that speaks lightly and immaculately to your soul . . . and moves her waves, thrusting to a splendid shore . . .
thrillsome and bathed in a beauty, untouched by words . . .
          Into the delicious darkness of a never-never land . . .
Rumors of a heaven . . .

Me and my American homie with slanted eyes, stoned by the springs of this kindness . . .

          Rain down on me your hail from high!

Let it go like a sigh . . . a breeze . . . come on to me . . . feeling you—feeling me . . .

My crazy wheat field of a child's soul . . .

          Sweet emergencies rain down on me!

                    Rain down on me like sweet ecstasy!

Pagan Paradise

God loves big asses.
                    I know . . .
          with an ankle bracelet to boot
around that thin feminine part of the body.
He loves the way her ass feels—getting bigger, blowing up in
size. Making the punishment of a possible rape most tolerable.
Little birds flowing out from the right cheek, in a flutter . . .
Walking down a paved walkway . . .

Rainbow

Light green foliage in this place.
This is the little sister's heaven.
Thrive its little melodic rainbow
in sunlight. Contrasting colors
of happy. Thrive.
Heaven waxes and it wanes.

Afghan Woman

I see flashes of an Afghan woman in the dawn of man; her image dancing icily like the fiery snakes of time, become a superfluity of children . . . wasting . . .
children . . . landed to waste . . .
children are a waste.

Her untouchable and desperate comeliness, like an old hag's, mesmerizes the human race with a forever forbidden lullaby.

I pay homage to this woman by lassoing authorities—which is my business. The great lake and its stories resound in me.

Could it be she, calling me at night through the stars? This freakiness that pulses in me like humanity's secret collective nightmares? Like someone's "weird scenes inside the gold mine"? Something to scare you out of your mind and senseless—forever, or for some time thereafter.

Alas, there is no home for me anywhere, but a mystery that cuts like a knife.

Untitled

We could be these boys like lithe tears rolling on the streets—boys, sketchily discovering our humanity with the weight of stars in soft pagan days' ebullience, where we had been etched as shadows, estranged shadows fallen under time's closed smile, under the smile's awry static of defending metropolises. We're fighters in the dawn against some ghost of glitter. Let this whisper of candidness float away from my syrup mouth with my eyes half closed like a dreamy moth in the month of June—capped in white gleaming snow . . .

I ever wanted coarse freedom—to leave my waste in gardens, to bat the tears of dew off heavy black birds' wings and follow their spiraling effusion of love into the torrents of everything

I remember like the sweet pearl crashing against the inside of my brain's tympem, of my carved center, this thought: what if God were the sum of our imperfections—like a strong day in our cities—a god with sealed-shut spontaneity and scorn for liberally flowing purity and love? I heard a little sister's beauty of words as drops of shining tenderness, explaining adult disapproval: "there's nothing wrong with chasing each other trying to tag one another with leaves of grass . . . It's just that sometimes people forget how to play . . . "

At the center of this creation's nerve of spiritual flowing redundancy I will bake for all and in the name of each one's savorable humility, a cake spun from our ties into flowing baby grass, and into the grass's pin echo of oceans in our hearing—the wisest, mildest rivet into the waterfall of divinity's black, choate heart . . .

Unconscious

Drip libertine serum on the tip of my cerebrum—coming at 5.56 on the dial—"¡Directo a tu cerebro!" Let me roll on, in the rooms of this youth storm, like the drizzle of an unknown electricity. Walking placidly down night streets . . . dream streets. Downing big Heinekens and Fosters like sweet foamy air. Strolling by antipodal shacks lining the road. Will these creatures and new bodies come out from under sealed doors, like insect realities? Like yellow Lamborghini tanks and their missiles pointed in peaceful harmony? A boxy, black sports car with a tootsie roll tint of windows rolls slowly on the street. Pray like rain for these nascent industrial flourishings . . . in a world of peons. Vanish! Florescence at the heart of the science of timeless youth's persistence and cool. This prayer for cool—calm and wild storm and electric . . . Ascend from the spiritual conscience of my heart!

Killing the Messiah

The villagers, my brethren, came like Klondike men from over the broken hills, beigely. "Kill the messiah," they shouted, "poison his hands," "set his wicker chair in flight with flame." So, with the help of my mother, we killed the messiah. He turned to gravel and a rope like a snake. "Leave him out to dry." The starry wind licked his spurs. My hair spoke of uncertain future.

They cried: "His daisies of lit brotherhoods are toiling in the can." He crawled down to the dark earth. He's like a book, like a brook, like a tomb, like a dream, wedged in the ground. We rocked the father to his frowning and shy foundation. Run, unsuffering children, from the pilfered places of the earth. "Mother," I say, "rose tea in the sky, we'll sip cup by cup." The dosification of the remedy bursts with it sundry suns. Rentable purple apartments burst with breakfast's warmth, its bleeding warmth. God bleeds from the cumulus clouds.

Sarah

My symbolic queen and prayer.
I love your dawning tiny feet
and lizard membrane, your
slivered sugar towers
without sparkle that take
a man's beige hand without
soft or firm affront . . .

Party Town

Women exchange glances,
attend to little men,
sending out this city love . . .

The Ancient Night

Apollo-calved,
I walked down pitch-dark street
of rotting city in lightest wear.
My soul arching into the ancient night,
piercing the mesh of slippery devils
and the soft, booming glory of bygone ages,
Looking for sex . . .

Light

I want to speak all the universe,
boiling in my membranes and deep valleys
of sprightly veins. Marmalades of misery
swooning in so many doctors' spirit and sport of negativity,
thrashing seraphim like hateful grannies detesting in the dirt.
Shout out the devils. Deliver us from the colonnades
of antiquity's Greek feeling vines, alternating in the pulse
of my machine of imagination. This awful violet light: blast
pleasantly. Let it ripen like some stinking Lucifer. Like a boiled
jewel, meat of sweetness. And all these newbies: the bit women
and their philosophies can bite the undertows under rocks.
The whole of this world and its river men and women:
go the way of waste and drown in the invisible course
of this thick current flowing underneath . . .

The Night I Met God

He brought with him a gift. The old man bid me give
him sweaty bills for his gift of daftly golden perfume,
sweeter than white dolphins. A perfume on the
brink of imperial seduction for a seed of a boy
grafted by heaven's pagan light. A boy met
only by some girls, the ones like wood demons.
The ones like fecund and curved ellipses . . .

Perfume, plunging in the vines of night and
the rippled pools of God's lithe face imprisoned
in summer. The face surfaces as a beige woman . . .
Perfume—imprisoned in crystal palaces that are
near and placeless and are woven from more
than the curls inside words. Palaces that
dripped transcendently from a white gold
ocean of God enshrined ghostlike in the perfume.
Body of lithest, flawlessly posing sea protected
in a glass bottle rubbing in the old man's bag
against the world. The bottle rubs against the
world's deaf and unlit items: the bag's plastics
and clothes. These are like softened children at
the threshold of knowing and not knowing;
their shoulders and hair defer to the glow . . .

The palaces refract their light through the melon
sundae heads of detestable youth wrapped in the
barbed wire of their graceful and pertinent rites.
Rites that arise from the spittle and light cud of
the youths' curved calculations.

Rites that rebel against their tiny imbecile stars growing weakly.

The youths' ignorance serves them well.

Perfume, worn, perhaps, around the necks of saviors,
the forgetful dames.

The old man who was God said
to dab myself in this liquid and
that he would turn up at my white
party in the darkest hour and tell
the ladies and everyone how much
he loved me. And, for seven
seconds, I felt how my beauty would
shudder into the dark night of their
pilfered wavelengths . . .

Rain

Hello means everything. It means I'm here and you're there;
it means I'm building a bridge between us, a possible heaven,
a calling. I brought this girl liquid gold on the rocks in
a sultry dark room and I secretly prayed for her
and knelt before her knees while The Doors
played, opening the door to every whisper and
cool sigh of riders in a storm. I felt her
presence and witnessed her feathered road and
calling through life. Somehow it was not credible.
We came to no climax and I saw her on her way
with a cry of the sun's liquid gold tears in my
pocket like farthings. We also had spoken of the prison
of self, and I quietly shouted my protest at this divination.

Why is it they choose pink wax over ovens of love?
Why do they choose glossy magazine pictures
over two butterfly sacred smiles and their stealthiest
and wettest kiss? Why is it they remember only for
three-hundredths of a second your out-on-a-limb madness
and disturbance of public composure? The disruption
becomes the liquid ring of a rippling wave.
The sonically fertile ring is imprisoned in the veil
of velvet tears of an immaculately bored race's dream.
The race is waiting for God's turnstile, for his bicycle.
Does God's face appear anywhere through the veil?

Heaven on Earth

For me heaven on earth is to irradiate Source.
Sweetly, ironically cursed, to lie on grass, fearing death
with a friend, but bathed in cool calm and a spirally perplexing existence
of life's bigger room of timeless freedom become the norm.
Heaven would be to smoke a magick and innocuous plant with
Jimena under crooked violet skies; and
to work part time in the day in a small supermarket nearby; this routine
would be my glazed happy mainstay for the time being.
I would lather my soul in seductive sex, feasting from time to time.
I would live in a hole in the wall and get high on a calm,
heavy, and harmless weed in a witchy girlfriend's room.
For me heaven is to be a part of this world and to attain the deep pleasure
of speech and thought and profound sanity, and to climb aboard a
leaf of inner safety, sprung from a knowing child's plainest words of
loving wisdom like a faucet dripping sweet soda. For me this
heaven would be to stir on the green with my father and rivet
him with a spiritual story or allegory
that would nascently dawn this eternity's soft, lime ebullience
in his generation's hard, adult body.

Radiation

I saw this girl. It's like she has no protection around her thin face. Her face flies so low and frail beneath all our steps and in the indifference of day's transfer to night. It's like she's enclosed in cold. It's like she's the inmate of an unknown and starless equation. I should be like a bird or God and put my arms through her blue halos and embrace them.

Equators imprison migrant birds like men. Padded melodies in the air come flying out to the birds, to rescue them and shuttle them halfway to infinity . . .

God has little toilers, deformed by right, that lunge into the horizon, where the world's tall fellows fall fast through the earth.

Ancient Kiss

I am this infant dreaming in its light brain
and creeping, sifting through soft palettes
like pages of tears stuck to the back of a star's contracted eye,
sifting through cream of naiveté and shores of thunder and
lightning exchange.
The infant knows I miss her . . .
"Mary." I never held her gaze in my palm.
The infantile naiveté, baby, being like an infantile universe,
microcosm pours in rivers, sonorous, through its head . . .

Quarter-life's naiveté knows sinisterly
(and the stars shout, raging out of their minds . . .)
The naiveté shares the world's letters:
of sleazy liaisons struck and purified by maternal breezes
like smashing waves of vernal semen; of meetings
where a man is softly struck by women with minds
like mouths, or like little apparitions in the air . . .

And there are infidel dogs and an
ancient one. He has a face with acquiescence of black eye.
Partly vagrant, at least three hundred years old.
Suffocating hills drip from my iris,
Olympian quiver. Wrinkles in the sun of Pompeii drown,
get doused before the tiara of next dawn sets her
lime sugar palace; before never rolls up its whole shadow,
or leaves a youth plum dead in red after a drive-by.
César died a medium stallion, half the way to early oldness,
standing on this pillar of limbo. Girls sweetly craved him.
He swore he could see so much with the world's almost
unbearable weight upon his fighting shoulders.
And in the last tide he threw his arms around Christ . . .
Dye the nether earth and the graphic streets
with the dying's light sense pouring from their split seams.
The ancient one drips, drips, and his crown laughs and smiles.
So, drink. Down. Drain the wrinkles' soft brain at dusk,

their wise

Empire . . .

Ingest this flesh. Get bereft of your view . . .

Dance on a liquid gold crown . . . in a dolphin's dream . . .

Swim into a man made of wink

Smoke an old man, dangle your limbs from the smoke rings for now. . .

Place the umbilicus of beings on a map . . . Laugh like a mad poet filled with light fire,

breaking well like a fly's inner light lighting up the face of a queen . . . Ever . . .

Everything has been done. Ride your will into the sky . . . Come cessation of talk.

Get the sky's appraisal . . . Travel there . . . Do what you need to do.

Gangs: Travel to the sun

kiss this masculine and warm man,

this numinous brightness

surrender your armies
your clothes
your sleek and
luxurious bodies

The Sound of Your Feet

In this lightly bound summer city, scattered across like invisible tides of sand, are these sonorous dreams and glazed whirlpools of plays. And one thousand plans, like elegant ethereal columns, in places—hovering. And a precious few surprises too. One little surprise, on whose shore I washed up one distant day like a spent, worthless gem or serpent become a curious and marvelous carved stone. Gathered at foothills of majesty's enthralled kingdom—lawless, agnostic kingdom of syrupy pleasures and brick red, lined hopes. And perfect pastiches in the sky—even higher than the glazed and whirled pools of spiritual endeavors and beauteous spontaneities. These laughing climes—softly derided by transient, laudable smiles clinging in the atmosphere. These: almost vulgar, through sharp, crackly pleasure. Smooth sail: cast away.

My heart, that day, was facing a brick wall and hurting. By cursed pantheons of Anglo-world, I had been stung blackly in the shoulders and navel heart of my spirit. Head down and sunk, but . . . all was known when, of a sudden, the sugary, watery tears yielded to elation. My heart spilling over in the sky and clouds, merging with the sound of your feminine feet in my soul. As yet too delicate to understand. A surf of sentiments so kindly, pleadingly real. The sound of your cutely miraculous feet, thundering gently in waves overtaking waves. Without an audible sound—only in these places in the sky. In the perfection of the summer day. Sounding softly like the peals of everyone's god or muse, unknown to them. City-earth humdrum soldiers pining in their uphill climb through valleys, far from kingdom's north shore. So down-to-earthly sublime: your feet, placed like an oceanic marbled prize, so sweet, in the glassy beige sky. One unheard musical note—so clear! Your small feet sounding in the temples of my soul!

Women

In the spearmint air of Eden through thispy slit eyes
I swam into the world—
where I effused sweet monsters in
the nursery, in the living room . . .

Kept the monsters out of the ladies'
star-flooded floor of wishful machination;
their modesty might have become mostly
wilted to wheat, to nightly waste.
Instead—having matured with the evening—
I will hide in the rivers and send your child-words
over the moon with my apparatus of music,
my golden-loaded machine of sweetness.
We can transcend laughter;
brush with Christ the stars—
imperishable pulps with mouths—
palpitating in the heavens . . .

I want to put the zenith of sex-suffused love,
effuse this point on the televisual face of your body
into the nectar of your creviced television—
waxing in the forests of my memory,
crashing against my membranes—
I look up to the skies for rain—
a sweet brainy child coded in crashing love.
Man-boy: communicate ethereal love to woman.
This silveresque gift in the prime of my existence.
Subsisting suns look up to skies for keys to Norse codes.
Motes separate our fusion—lightest, lithest stings—
come from your willowy wiggles.
Dance forever and ever in these woods; in these glades;
in these super peals of some manifest kingdom—
I once heard . . .

These City Streets

These city streets at night plead with me to voice
their time-swept beauty as they echo their gravely
street-lit story stretching far into the night . . .

In their gravel, in between, lives my joy—the spirit of life . . .
In the air: a myriad fractured sparks and dreams that got
discarded with time . . .

But these streets echo on . . . swoosh! Far into the night . . .

And where some see sick lantern light, I inhale love.
Where they see desolation, I hear the city streets'
echoing of the Golden Age—pleading with me to voice
their time-swept story as they echo their gravely
street-lit beauty stretching, far into the night . . .

Baby

Whirl me in your sundry Lego heavens;
whirl me in this wine of a weak graduate's smile
of a weak person's ecstasy, of lovers' shy
effulgence of shared sunlight—trailing
of slippery piano keys in air, lighter than
fingers and the frozen intentions of man . . .
Slippered ghosts. Fluid trumpet,
outbound partial prayer of gold and
wistful wheat-soul—melted,
creased humiliation follows at dawn;
and then: mobilizing smooth
chartreuse armies in their wake,
in sweetest revenge . . .

Raucous Voice

Smiles of teddy bears,
dripping down by whims of children
The teddy bears are softly fighting
and darkly dancing in the snug of night . . .
Parade of rain of laughing plane
hurray the jungle gym and its bells
and the laughing brain of the rain

If

If I could talk to trees and God,
If I could drink with the devil in bars,
If I could seduce women,
If I could listen by the seed of history's
timeless echoes in the ancient night,
If I could discover underworlds,
physical and spiritual,
If I could own a mansion
and willingly sleep in the streets,
and if I could travel to the sky,
do you really think I would
bother to write even one word?

The Andean Flower in London

Rock it! Spray it all across your jeans . . .
        Summer city . . .
Future's London radio: dock at portals of resilient love. Shirts ripped in the style . . .
        Gorgeous songs at Number 1 for seven weeks . . .

But our story begins somewhere in 2001–2002

Still no shaded downtown stalls from which to sip eternity's pleasantness yet . . .

Wake to sumptuous 10 o'clock morning . . .

Manacled softly, as in a dream, to morning and softly crying, leaking city . . .

No vent for frivolous or deep affection in the sealed crater of such a taut town.

Sighs get their bottomed-out bellies torn against the city corners

        and the tarmacs

        underneath

They don't even know . . .

Nip the buds of my love—sinking and singing their deafened song by white gargantuan belchers chasing around the corner in the street.

Nobody knows . . .

My sticky essence breathes sweetly from the wealth of parental house on the shores of Chelsea, and I know . . .

The city sparkles with the luster of golden ages in our imminence . . .

On to uni . . .

. . . and back. No one cares. Passersby oblivious in their feeding stream.

Portending. Robotic, suspended street lights guide their intuition and free their frazzled Anglo brains. And mirrors flash their souls. I dream for the bridesmaids' sake . . .

City strangers . . .

. . . Lay off my heart! You anchored mothers, manacled maniacs, or whatever you please . . .

In the streets are clammed-up women, and girls with zipper hearts jaded by national horrors and the living mediocrity of living days—obfuscating their soul . . . They pass me by every way . . . They and everyone are nothing but greasy burger buns on a conveyor.

Have it not your way . . .

Ready for swirling canopy of beauty. Down the tube our heavens went. Held up a crippled hope to reach to the sexy greenish stars staring down and grinning at the melting death of our souls . . .

Still I carry this northern glow of quixotic torch . . .

This sumptuous lunch undressing in the lilac sun . . .

Fragrant makossas

Where Andean and white and black essences of bodies intermingle

and diffuse my spirit in these talking brains and jeans of city, of northern dying,
cycling city . . .

Exotic mango. Big, sexy-assed, cumbersome. Odd fragment of jeweled lewdness. This prankster . . . This weak creature . . . Trammeling colts carry this shy boy forward. Misbehavior in scooter and car land with a fragile son of bitch . . .

. . . Shaman, ugly freak, caved into world and useless like a silver can drooling and spilling on the ground its sound history of meager, miserly flowering . . .

Heighten your praises for a melodious prince, an invisible demon, singing what you're unaware of . . .

A beauty from afar with a perfection and a body light as a miniature perfume bottle . . . Nasty, English buildings sway away in their foul petrifaction of carnal heroes . . . Sway away like a foamy ocean!

My sexiness breathes plenty divine in London city.
Shore up this insolent, scornful beauty when
touched the wrong way . . . this quixotic beauty
pivoted from

dark terrain, flowing over from warm brown
mountains . . .
. . . He's comical too.
Can you hear the Andean flower?! Broken over the hills.
The new surreal American—
vivifying

the town and people in this way . . .

Lay off my heart with your Anglo-headism. Your cube-headed machinations . . .

Lay off my heart!

In the din of fruitless, loveless lands, didn't your parents, your people, teach you to touch?

Pour Adam in the water supply!

Let me spiral this man's voice up and sing
fluorescently, yearning in cascading ecstasies: "Lay off

my heart!"
Some women could sense this beige and light-green, playful
magic of sexy thrills, of sunbathers and divers beyond stars and
touch . . .
Our bodies could breathe for one another for moments
. . . Our naked feet . . . talk and touch without moving . . .
A heady sweetness on the point of a big burst

Be brave for big sensuality.

Just for a pause . . . A lightning sizzle . . . An island of light . . .
of
flight . . .
. . . Back to home alone

this fragile fragment

this supernal dancer

dancing alone!

Little Poet

Praise be to bloody knotted tribes, entranced. And all the swarming of human thronging and thrusting. And newspapers rolled up like baseball bats with their swindling batters. Poets booming the horsemen of their times and ages with thinly veiled criminality of niceness. Poets with their horse-hoof minds and hollowed heads with lackey veins and gas hearts. And, perhaps, a set of keys—figuring as trembling premonitions of long finger touch to piano, or the inside of glass slippers, where "what man does makes him so, so much larger than this": the stars scream nervously. And hide in their near invisible winking, the knowledge of a key's slide into queen of hearts' silky night-havens, sublimely lit up with their luscious secrets—held tightly by the matron haters—hateful like murderous knife stabs. And I see devils floating across streets and folded women's legs thrown by a dusty town side street. And all the sinners in ambered dense glow of eternity and saints. Killers and soft steppers tip-toeing over fragrant glaciers in their cause-heavy night and life of glowing incandescence and after-thought . . . And the soft speakers like mini oracles—oozing into atmosphere. Rubies blasted through a humungous organism that is like a hairy container of all men's doings and dreams and long-threaded thoughts—connected to the heavens. And I see men languishing in seasons of fire and nocturnal recess. Also, men frozen in light, despairing vespertine sorrow of suddenness, suspended in limbos, skipped across water surfaces like long flint pieces. In evening, I walk down a street by spread-out university grounds, where a silk-skinned young woman with books walks femininely to class, in fiery flip-flops, with a trace of a dirty smile. My soul licks the air around her and wishes upon the vast and all-highest connections of things. Men will shed tears like sparks. Some may speak for lacquered and fecund forests of black misery. Others will speak for pools of oil—destitute like logos gnomes and frozen shadows and weird cars with scary parties rioting inside. See that wired smile in your skull. Still, other men—with the super hubris of niceness bursting from their gall of vested chests—will speak and write of cranes and their candied sweet heights—reached with saccharine tears and curlings of iron weights by these strength-deprived young men with their feeble minds. These men abdicate all but the thin wisp of noose of secret heights—now chambered away. A ship that knocked into indigo rocks of despair. There are wizards with skullcaps in castles for this poet who has lost the little skies. He has been rung down dream ladders. Poets are rewrought and hurled back down to earth—to be vomited out. Poets wrought from nights' sleeves. Poets that surface to streets' alien lamp-heads and turgid whirlpools of machination—machinating in the viscous knife of night. There are the losers abounding with untied laces. Oracles spin from cleanness of street. And a woman sweeps the street's sweet misery, and its dust—with desperate memories screamingly clinging—uprooted from the warm sparkling stretch of the night street's bosom.

White

Give me almond essences blistering in the sun.

Give me the world's children.

Their steely infant hearts are snowed in by the sun's slumbering words.

A precious molecule snowed in.

A molecule like the device of a tube that is for cleaning ears, for gushing blue, for soft molding of tender electronic art installations. A tube for lifting teeth a shade of white.

Bright children and half-surging princesses are semibeautiful, so becoming in their buoyancy of every day's hard crests of lifting clamor. These endangered children and their mothers. Their defeat is in the loud and abysmal crashing softness of cloth. And their stars are breathless, reeking numbers. I pray for the horse that is their dream and god. They drip as brown syrup into superman's dimple, louder than baseball . . .

I love to know and feel these absurd persons. I radiate the quiet echelons of their white God. And I exchange the cursed, thirsting unbreakability of daylight for the liquid packets of their coagulated thoughts.

Sundays wash up on their dirty money. Sundaes glaze their heads, spearing their hearts that flesh out cool lies with the eyes of lizards . . .

My heart and her kind hair rally through the wheat fields of their words and stopped hearts . . .

And a kind of God, intent on distracting, feeds me glazed donut for my compartmentalized brain whose "here" festers, unable to fly through gates . . .

I would fly lighter than birds' nests tearing violet pools
sounding the gutters
of adult observers' downcast eyes . . .

But I would die to enter the white toilet kingdom of the sweet designs' desire.

Stray Sister

Please expend my innocence
through the world at its cost
in breathy glory. Because I
am the indigo sliver of a
jagged key into a shy cat's essence;
puerile and unchaste effulgence in
a purple dame's iris—liquid gel
in thin-stranded symbiosis
with the spidery suns and the
light-green diving stars . . .

Flowers

Dogs knock at the doors of trees: “Let in our furred hearts. Let us bloom to morning;

. . . to the prophet . . . ”

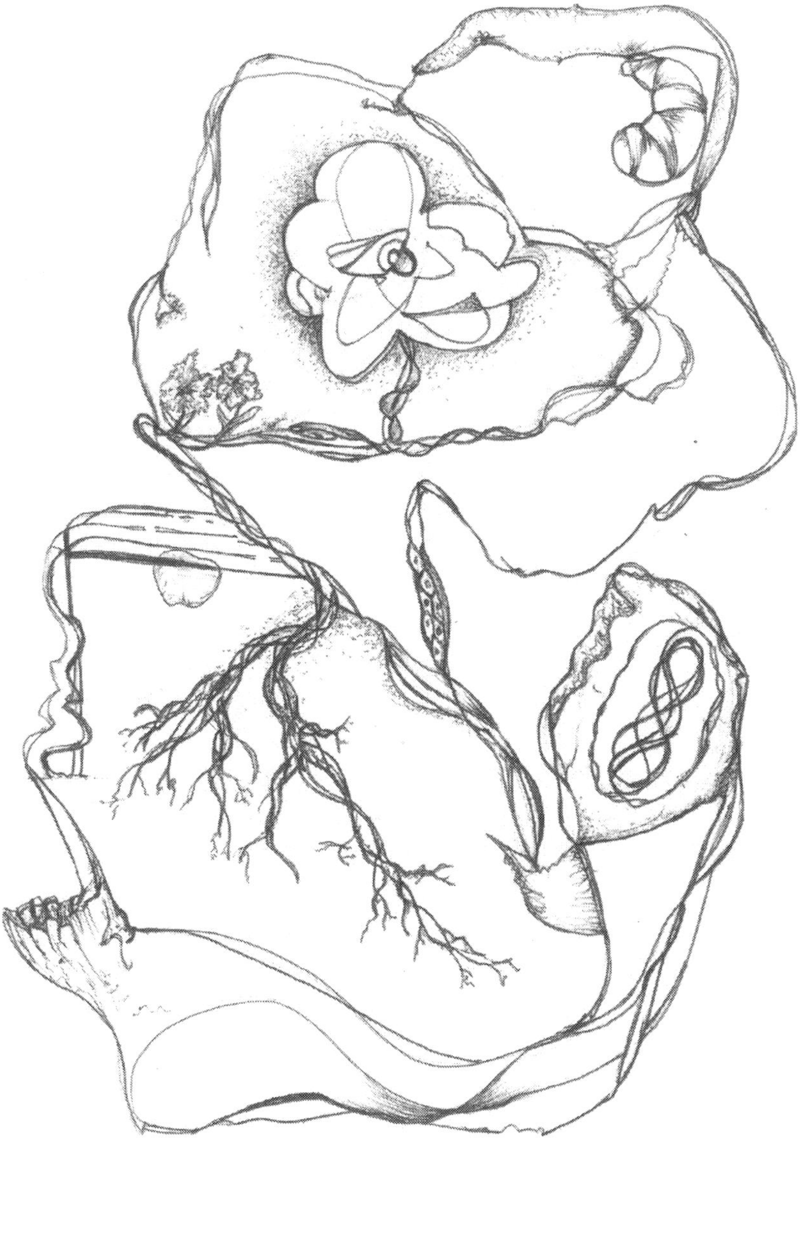

Red Hindlight Epidemic

Cars' red sick jewels, like sinking to city lights in cars' motions to city, like offal waves to purple-blue rock . . . And dizzy music of peaceful insanity dazzles. Candied embers incipient in a global headache; tirade—tour de force of curtained glow; ever lower than surfaces; lower than streets and walks; welling up from crocodiles' insipid toy-fire eyes; like a thread running through programs' loopholes. And dentured wise men serve us life through clear glasses of whizzing water, like spring sex sprees in dreams with springs. The curtains and floating glow of this epidemic, welling up from primality, run through the universal of demo-cracy mode-s and fine lines of rationale and absurdness of mysticisms, and going at veins in discussions, like walking backwards—shrinking—sillily, or swindling down drains. Play with night's red lights cascading over our implacability of hair, welled forth from prisons of silence like stolidness; and icons—dashed—their loudness . . . Red glows—like sugar falls on deadbeat diabetics—seeping in simmering richness like pelts of summer spoils sacking winter's realism with primal-suffused beau of springing new, from long yearning down: in siren of yellow jax lights tumbling in spinning motion over truck, with their syrupy slops waning in far ears. Trucks with so much the richness of Good Humor men—broadcasting this vein in their mortuary night of incandescent splendidness. The sirens—sweeter in some men's souls than candy floss to girls in summer fairs. Red candy light—sweeter than women that roll . . .

Monkey Shampoo

Let violence sway my sun. The flutters of that baseball boy are clipped in a gun under the sea of children's beckons to the sweet rushing heaven of falling forever into the toes of "Let's go play . . . " Outside in the summer. Dandelions save the day. Their broken crystal neck cracks in the low-flying sky. Homework finishes like icing put on a cake. And the sea of beloved green moves its shore to our desk; at least to the front door where we see our noble and laced shoes beaten down by the rain and scythe of play . . .

With these marble marvels of adults' tentacled supervision like buses and rainbow skin of beetles—ain't nobody got to stop the sea outside. The streets flow in butter. And time has knocked back its black and dirty monkey hand of ridicule that always meddles with its hurt and worse than whimpering . . .

I sound with the bursting diamonds in the air,

the best ever in the expanse of days curled like a savior's lips

Give me foreplay with dolphins

Outside I listen to the greed and some Moses
surfs the green; it's his hazed daughter, his hazed play crashed
into the melted butter wings of the playing streets' angel . . .

I wish for this light massive span of wings in my blood-letting day . . . My laboring under rainbow men and mighty steel superstructures deafening the speeches of my inner person . . . His person's tongues swim in the Pacific calm . . .

Many pretty Martians get slaughtered . . .

Give me the manifest monkey shampoo of childhood.

Give the sweet whiff of play

and somersaults . . .

Give me streets that say something,

soaked in grey and visible letters of lightning poets who love the superstructures

Give me conversations with the rain . . .

Rinsed of all cares and conventions, ragged, I wade in the street

before the gaze of all—

this pelican desire,

this flaking and hopeless

brown-beige monster

moving slowly,

ravaging their sandwiched thoughts . . .

Bubbles

A man sits upon a chair in the middle of an American back yard—enthralled, liquidly light, with arms extended in this some kind of afternoon breakfast of some kind of energy with big bubble waves coming, crashing down onto his arms and chest and face. I, ethereal child, poised on the wonder of big women, sense and almost spy his living ghost from the next door house's back yard where I mingle with friends and families. No known god treads the sky. Has the man heard in his head this song played one hundred and three times? Or, at least, a white sliver of the song imprisoned by him in a contrail in his brain? It's an American thought descended on this thin and wiry Ken. These beige rays, crashing as waves, like an answer to afternoon's and all days' light burning desire, a misplaced thirst—in need of beyond what is proffered by the frigid sacredness of the frail old man who goes by the name of radio and gestalt. Once, long before, it seems, with coolness, I had argued on variations of themes with the enthralled man in the back yard.

Cursed Shore of Star

Neptune's feminine tyranny
of oceans scatters across lore's lone staircase.
And his blue steeds with carriages,
shards of sublime navies and armies
—shatter into night—
burst forth from the prison-vest of sky
like lonely and insane stone icons
granted wings in the first streaks of the sun's death.
Copper fields, wings lulling in my beige pastures
"Mother . . ."

wake to flight—calm and somber.
Flanked by wings, steel wings, mockingbird wings
dip low into a.m. sun,
dip naked Christ in the blue

Cry

Revere

All be done!

I cease to stir in day

recall the silence of my parents in departing.

Maybe I will die gracefully, and maybe
I will stir softly before the sunset's soft parade
with the prism girls released from prison.
And the ghastly gold palaces shivering and dying in cold.

Horses are instrumental in the art of cold.

Crete is blazing. The minotaur's maze is at my
shoulders and, yet, looming below and beyond horizon.
We've exchanged bloods, and my black eye reads space
treading in a land made from hay
such a crossfire . . .

Fury dangles like a knife from the myopic green moon

The dames' glass slippers are strewn and defeated on the
ground . . .

And the world appears to be ours. It is, but a quivering
white silk cloth at our feet . . .

And away from the blazing cry of the world,
sitting on a log in a field, is old Napoleon—
with his sword in the ground
and his head sunk in hands.

Here, on this old log,
in this sea of grass

his soul waits for the cold phantom before dawn . . .

Lover

Listen: I want to listen and breathe
by entities woven from electrical rainstorms,
through the haze of vexation and irascibility,
and I want buttery suns of dripping holocausts
and rainbows in a black pan.
I want the people to defend themselves from
the invasion by a follower of some illusion.
I will watch people playing their safe, soft games—
whirling a while. I'm building sacred nets
for myself and scared-sacred friends,
feasting on the gods' playful bile in the
mustard and white clothes of night—clothes
of softly gawking lady, softly driven,
with overly enterprising speech, mauve-brown
orchid—in an airport, where I met her.
I touched her fabric and laughed softly
with acquiescence, and I left her and loved her.
I love weird ones; wired to thrills of talking,
with minds that are heavy like planes and thunder . . .

They're old saplings.

They are friends living in the pulsing
          and short flight of this song I know,

                    that's like a breeze into God

Youth

I wish that I could close my eyes and slip
into the heart of youth with its beauty.
Moveable feast of youth and warmth of becoming
　　　　under the docile stars.
Coming up from under
in the stairwell of a house party
and through the open balcony.
I'd sit with her on the ledge,
and she would look at me with her sixteen years
　　　　of knowing,
her curled hair wisping back with the wind.
I would stare back at my goddess of her time—
　　　　smiling at me.
And everything would be okay, because I too
　　　　would be beautiful—
with my seashell choker wrapped around my neck . . .

Not Stars

Why do you stay in me, burning ember of disconformity? Light chalk of hated teacher and prophet's branding word. Over me are rivers emitting happy smiles and sorrows. Over me are the sweet hurrahs of welcome backs and mild, inner calms of common days. The little calms remain dotted and scattered along towns where a shy virgin or a duller girl carries out domestic duty.

She said: this staring in the city street must be put to rest.

This energy of love does not belong here.

So, I try to get lost in the brown din of their voices like dried leaves. Suspend their world at the level of my hearing. Still estranged . . .

Sometimes, I can almost hear.

I must learn social gravity. I must learn the fast switch of words.

I'm going to suck the warmth of words.

First, I'll seek and find acts that smell of teenager to help me through the cold galaxies of the numb family, the loving kin. Their instrumental song smells of breathless numbers, burning wavelengths and emaciated wicks of being . . .

Artists often get sucked into dense goo of eyes. But, I chose the lighter route of fire. Fire's eye molds my floating, falling-apart limbs in this layered universe. Fire keeps me warm and glowing in the cold, cold universe, in the transition and in the padded, cold, melodic xylophone of exiting.

I'm going to suck the warmth of words.

I walked down into the cellar, down melodic steps that are big piano keys across. I kissed an image of what behemoth of a fetus I can't say or hear. A nocturnal creature of burning orange skin. The film was called: "The synthesis of night's and day's most miniscule desires and contact, the tints in their glasses." I was at a breath to disclose, to disguise under the dew, under the smooth and light-gilded nations of my fingernails, the strangeness of parents . . .

Still, I must learn to relate better socially. I went to official routes . . .

I gave up my brains at the prefect and yelled aloud. Alas, I was given this flask with a scented word. Words of suavity: hear my chant, the trembling caress of the brain of my voice. Send the teacher couple the words of lavender design. Words, left beached, in sweet basking. Ask him and her whys, holding a bag of nails. Send me micrograms of piano keys for the words' sleep. Touch the notes, touch and slightly turn their noses. Ambrosial skies effuse from the noses' long pores speaking. This importance of the words slides down poles.

Born is this message of finicky word to blow over the world.

Light chant, light rant from the brained skies. There are little lightnings in the word's cuticles. Its brave coasts of soap of lathered affection circulate the ethereal diamond of your heart. I blow into your gathering atriums. My columned friends are now calmly stranded, away from me, but with the appellation of this threaded ovule of parent.

We have larger parents in the world than the alien cotton swabs of letters. In dreams I could twist a rusted dagger into her, but in the surface of day I laugh through parades with this mother. Then there's the rushing sprints of love . . .
And the empty American homes full of childhood's and E.T.s' ghosts in the thick air. Woman, perpetual mother: unfold your bowers of roses and their redolent, red perfume. Build us a paradise from your soft clowns. The dripping fire of children's voices. I love the tenderness and gently anticipate the oncoming ride that is heavy when the vault of our heaven cracks a little open.
Show us a way into the garden of your magick, of burning spearmint engulfing sky
and planes
and counting girls' fingers.
In the contrails of their effete and plump fingers there is a love for the big family. There is a blasting blue fountain of sweet-tinged pain, a tinged staircase to small, clumpy paradises of little people and to varnished white skies of peculiar mercy. And

there are tides of creatures speaking their soft and curious languages . . .
. . . closely . . .

Everywhere people walk, blind to everything, except a silhouette—emitting their reason for being like a sprinkling flower lamp that thinks and cries in the morning . . .
These persons are large-brained doves.

Silence chimes
gently three times.

Let me write "I love you" with blue finger paint on your human chest in this moment, on your warm, slowly burning father's chest.
I wait for the world. For these big-faced and silent old heroines in the elevator. These loved and cared-for women wrapped in concern. I stare from behind the bars of their enzymes at their sullen eyes and braced contours. I focus beyond my insulted starling—a tear. I come and look close to their eyes, milking their miniscule mechanisms and relishing in my breezed rush through a finish line, with the swooshing rain of the sky-brain Bra-zil!!!
I rest my legs and heart in the yielding brains of these hopeful, gurgling candy loves breezing over radios. Broadcast of girly youth . . .
I must believe that we're better off than anyone could imagine.
If I could take this secret from the sky, I would . . .
For this precious and ultimate secret they would leave my tortured body turned over high in the air.

Archway

Lilting above the black
dissonance of the streets, I'm this warm
pillar of flesh with lime green center

I'm this beacon pouring
out its light like a weak father in
search of kindness

Wipe out the negative souls
with the soft cruelty of killers,
with the seraphic beauty of cowboys
in dawn's highway, like roses
Boys linked by mile-long veins
to the mothers with special care

Build a fire
from God's eyes

from the devil's rigs

Sunrise War

Father flows dead through the river.
Tongues splay forth from his body,
whispering the engineering secrets
of his dark and frozen house, zooming by,
in flight, overhead; of his resting
seraph-home; of his beloved peace,
streaming out of the home's high
windows; shreds of warm tigers;
warring clusters of causes,
carried by the wind. The house,
like a sauna, brims over with special peace.
Ravage me, father, with your medicine;
doctor a mind and show me the fluid light
of elves laughing by savage and nice night's dawn.
His essence dawns seraphic,
expending night.
Father—from translucence—to God.

Father, grant me your consent . . .

I wish to marry gold
and blow from a cliff,
a tender wish with the helios
figments of a dandelion

. . . and the clouds shall shed pink tears for my sake . . .

Cry

We often get compromised with radiant, earthly mentors. Their hollowly echoing melodies turn to silly, mellifluous streams. The streams flow uphill with our copious natures that are like sweltering rocks—champion slaves—with cryonic chests of gold-horror. The slaves' minds are like mines and animals; where would-be absinthe tasters look for lopsided café drinking. And, perchance, science can start to accrue in man's gateway to pleasure and the stars. Men drenched in bosomy women all over in a black room. Minds in the sun's heat—beaten down like trails of teary natives, rubbed together like sassafras souls—surfing souls of large-bodied women fed from the earth, river, and sky. She's sleeping in the whole of a field-clearing in the woods; where, elsewhere, we'd shy away from a zillionth of their Crimean pristine. The universe is in the severity of a pin dropping. Locomotives were the willfully violent action appeal to our finest and most awesome future-building. There is a vertically ethereal God inside towering youth with molded atheist minds—get taken in a storm of universal rhyme scheme, throwing winds and disks and padded points into the thronging crowd usurping this flashing genius, speaking to the stars and world centers. This is the end. Stalinist night of vast podium, vaunting over absent audience. Nightmarish comedy of our father. Stars litter the curtain, swung open. Let's lisp and sleep to the tune of whistling pines and the soft musicality of the stars, drizzling the love of their manic tears, sent from way outside. This supernal melodic pulsing, exclaiming and hitting the atmosphere of our hearing again and again like estranged, delicate ecstasy of white soul surfing its way into cities of angels. There must be these other-sided dawns where we're all these immaculate young people, landed upright, gathered around pools of sunset, drinking this vine of song—our dance, universal—where we're frozen in armed forces and stone beauties. Recollecting where a Danny-boy wilted tears of small sorrow on a bed at the death of a friend. We were this trenchant smile, a smiling ghost that passed through a decade. People stared at our striding through streets, god-loved.

Further I fall behind vinyl cataracts and their warmth, like personalized tub rides within time's or space's shedding of amorphous house dreams; it's like the cry of a little girl. And the distant, cold musical sound of steel girdles—not of city, but of endless kingdom. Our soul falls with this motion at careless dusk with the looks of a little girl and fatuous love, like a notion in the air . . .

Huge laned parks, languid and disturbed in long-haired, green composure,
with creaking little houses at their zenith. Flow through: creeks and fascination, wrapped within and up winding stairwells. The floor below last's stairwell has paintings, schemes like faces, traces of secrets in blurred bubbles and soft-colored magazines—rich with dusty maneuvers. These—never uncovered in everyday or dreams . . .

A decrepit sailor's fiery blue eyes

Moving house . . . Isolated castle. Island house . . .

Barking moons. Biting moons . . .

I woke from my nap to remember my pact of trust with a familiar sister. She was like a little, weak, and resilient flower—exonerating in this strange and calm planet where I awoke alone with this strange sound of music. This desert of sound and expectancy. Going through drawers, big and small, in the timeless late afternoon. My little Asian sister; my little rock or shell; my little link . . . Where there is little love and everything is a question of trust: splayed out as little lasery sun rays over a shimmering sea . . .
The sea tells of our peace. Breathe back into us warmth of man at peace . . .

Bring us more than the faint rumors. Send us the shimmers of a great life. Teach us the science of mature love and happiness. Take off the clothes of our sorrow. Draw our minds on the ground with a stick. Drown our minds in the seas of pink and naked childhood. Far in.

I see carnivals and kaleidoscopes and merry-go-rounds and indelible grape-painted realities and fogs like a heaven's shudder or blowout of powder, of power. We rise to mountain tops by helicopter, and it was little less than enough to have smelled animals in the night. You could see a whirl in the sky of the world, and poetry is ever a quivering figment fashioned in all manner of everydays, like a camera flash. And none realizes what poetry is, like an electrical storm. And almost no one understands . . .

I can almost swim and hear to some Atlantis through the mirror glass. Atlantis's pulse pounds on the dock of my chest and veins like a brain . . .

Like a spiritual muscle . . . Neither needed nor needful. Playthings dangle from my large, camouflage tree-being—rocketing violently through brawny, star-filled space; it rockets in flight and lukewarm; in this strange and calm clime of space. And, beyond, I see our entire world and race unlocked from a keyhole through a teardrop. As boy, I'm hunted in great musty blue where the virile and tender song of me rises and throbs of our love; in a cruel and offending universe of darkness. And flashing black action.

Journalists storm the grates with their black hundreds of digits like fists and inky veins, secretly pointing the way into overcast, aching skies and their Colombian whispers . . . I wait for the island where hurt ever melts like flowers. And the entrance into the luxuriance of my dreams of rocking isles, azure speeded with colorful blasts of sweetness, like the raw blue of children's tongues dyed by blow-pops—

come swiftly swans . . .

Invisible Rain God. Invisible rain of God: Pull me into your ebbing tides of peace like silver light, like a silvery lie conquering me from within, crippling the day and woody trees with this natural shadow and manic Barbie dolls, peeled like sex toys. The world is an abomination because of lack. Nuclear profusion. Nuclear holiday. So many banana loves yet to be and wrenched documents spruced out their doves of fecundity. Over us: the soul of an animal or spirit, thrown over our vision and hearts in rotting sky. That we might have poets for forecasting. Give is a blowout. Give our embered chests a blowout, extinct to a hard place. The embers are like leaves' edges painted with dewed light. The dewed light is like prismatic happiness and the icing of violins. Here everything is simple and soft as dying. Let us walk, rising up to the street and making this moment of contact with splendorous afternoons, racing against mountains on green emerald-surrounded highways. We're like families with college minds sinking into further up sundowns of silken vibration of electronic hearkening. Our chastity of soul is topographically demarcated in our minds in this enthralling kingdom of music that only says: "God is great."

Make this crumbling hall of love where we're with our race . . .
Make a peace in me and all and my home; make my silky certitude like a bed. Lift this shower of darkness of sorrow. Where creeks and rivers undress naked in my mind . . .

A clandestine meeting between mother and son. . . A love encounter. . . Like the time you threw a pebble into the water and you and she watched the miracle of the ripple . . . Spread us across the faces of time . . . so magnified . . . and magnified . . .

Let our freedom echo and linger like a soft petal in the temples of beginners . . .

Tomorrow and forever . . .

Faucets

Big faucets drip silver rivers and drops—flush the nuisance of my waving brain and knocking caricatures—and flow, flow like the cars—rivers horizontal/vertical, south—along yellow walls. There are also imagined white beaches partitioned from fluid sight. All abound. All the ants and cracks and supine necks of sparse trees rehearse, and all odd and old objects break apart. Flushings and sprockets of poetry—in thin atmosphere of Andean city. The rivers are plenty and awash with silver trinkets molded by this pale, liquid day.

Malignant men, like pin-up flowers, move along; these were the insignificances that made me nervous where I had to be cloistered away—listening for stirs in the air, for the break of curtains . . .

Paradise street is long . . . with a woman's disembodied legs folded by roadside and white rock in these towns with their myrtle music coming from out of the cracks . . .

Olivia

Whirl me in the magic of the
melodic light of the light
falling of the leaves.
Blast for fun, my native
black-faced guards . . .
tired worms . . . clod-footed
sentries without smiles—
Rush past their tearing gates
of sundry suns of mute defiance—
with a hurricane of purity,
and leave me in almost no
hatching sense on the sidewalk,
softly destitute, with my self-serving
neighborhood—sounding sweet-sister's echo.
Breathe in this experience in the light beige day.
Colors trickle back like boys and board games
into new view, hiding with the watery-tiered
memory of reality. And, lost, I could almost
remember, little sister, when you peeled
big tears from off my eyes,
and I blew into your shore—freed in spirit . . .

Horse Flower

I come back, again, to lightly flail the old horse of days. An undissipating mind, still, knows or contains nothing, not much. There is no king in my blue kingdom. There is no serpent tamer in these precincts. I don't look anymore for my soul in the lake of other eyes and faces, those placid pools of vanished cherishings. Wise friends in the making slide down and around my fingers. I had thought they were only orange sand; it seems they are doorways to pulsing planets with hexagonal, sand-blasted queens. The phone is ringing. Still, I'm neighing to my nerds and fans about the black shiny sphinx of our dreams. Our daughter is a thin Clarke at our heel; she's ever one inch behind us. The emperor's silver car is born from her. I am this hose, this emerald baby snake, like a toy of finished and sharpened essence. The viper has climbed into the choate countries of your thoughts; it is coiled like a centipede in its still center; it is wrapped around like the icing of graceful nerve; and it is running through the nations of your palms that are like green, wide-faced leaves . . .

Exetal

This ecstasy of sunshine of meadow bursts over the hills of my dreams, billowing from far way. This nice sun god blows through blue highways. Soar through the pool's hallways, floating with dripping memories of boys, these nothings. Nothing was ever as bright as a white, shining rainbow and laughing, languid sighs in the clingy azure atmosphere. This view is for you, my darling, your side glowing orange sunlight beside the rivers' courses. We're rinsed of our homework and infinite care. Nothing we ever did, little sister, of my white bringing could have brought us as close as that wide Sunday sun, perched on joyous tears and sunny freckles and splendid sun dances through porches in the serenest summer where your purple dance covered my fright-imagined fears and old-as-mountain breath. We could dive like purple dolphins into the grainy sand of our invented parents. Sweet seed of sunshine, come, bursting our dreams. And there is this daughter of tiny, searing fountain that they couldn't hassle. The miracle of verdure of sweet syntax propels her baby feet forward; she's a quaking giant over the years of light pain and hustle and raspberry hollows. Give us the perfume of the cologne of the trees and their wise visions. The trees come bursting my blue dreams that are like sleeping elephants. There was a saccharine turbine in my ears when she dug into the memory of little boy humiliated, and I learned how she had softly ruptured tears for him from her little-girl heart as she lay tucked in the temperate nectar of her bed on the white-blessed school night, breathing the softness of her little-girl feelings, the nicest color-crystal verities of a tenderized love. If only she could have handed the night a white small hand, but it was not to be. You know how much I love leaves of grass, frozen steeds of summer. And you know how I wished for divine forgetfulness of peaceful and illicit rest, which is why I'm writing you this letter with doting words and pictures, that perchance you may fix my face over highways and recall how I rarely fit the treadings of fellow men, but clumsily leafed through the sheets of your soft blue and caramel kindness.

Kathmandu Chain

Where is this special girl to throw my arms around as though I was a diver, and kiss her lotus lips and be swallowed into her cosmic mouth? I am the suffocated hills of pungent spirit. She is my universe, dressed in advancing everydayness and a ray of Arab beauty and sexiness. She said she didn't like the smell of wine or beer. Vodka was nice, clean and voluptuous, and also: coconut . . .

Barren spoils of European city . . . Stand in front of the pain—largely looming and these bastard, pilfered cars machinating in daytime luxuriance of metropolitan hospitality . . .

The east could be my remedy for futile boredom and progression of flaking soul and mind. This surfacing of desire without remedy. Seeking everywhere: the doors that lead to sumptuous sanity and flexing vein of inner effulgence that outwardly displays itself as: my American planes crashing down onto wet streets with "Julio and me down by the schoolyard," near the basketball court, in the heavy summer . . .

The kids scooter away . . .

Take the ghoul's dive into the eastern prison which is the universe's greatness, its infantile susceptibility to nice minds—seeking contact with colors and cubes and wonders that glow as day. Seeking what should be the norm and standard of spiritual curiosity . . .

. . . its shadows and bicycles and

astronauts

. . . its lysergic dreams

. . . and dreamy wheat fields . . .

Through streets of Kathmandu that

swallow handsome

lean Europeans with hippie hair… Their reverb pours through my dreams and machinations . . . I—pulling at their oceanic hair like goldfish dropped in a pond, within a prism, within a shrouded
fantasy-dream . . .

. . . and Nepalese, Asian men,
drily drunk,
flanked by their foul friends,

tidily taking them away . . .

. . . neither good nor harm be done;

Do the drunks' insidiousness resound like coming feedback—
from over the purple hills of the Andes . . . ?

Being that we're all tied together—

We dyed the Andean intuitions in purple fluid . . .

. . . A girl called Maya cried: "reality is overrated."

Could culture, then, be annihilated?

And we'd walk on the rubble of our thoughts staring up at precious, naive skies . . .

But, feel this invisible cosmic ocean . . .

With its lassitude of benign magnitude

And malevolent devising, villainous peace wrapped in:

solid skies and cloud . . .

This special, sparkling indigo sea that spills: that delivers:

The secrets of Shiva and his ride down to earth on a Majestic bull, in the massive warehouse-temples of eternity—where things and appellations are surreally big and formidable . . .

And the sweat is gold . . .

All the Asian girls could shove rice from the street into their little mouths . . .

They could be fed the violet, savage equestrian secrets of a better day, growing up like stalks through the cracks; and, one day, on through the roofs of men's minds and ends . . .

Give them the secrets they deserve—sleeping in their watching spirits . . .
that speak and move through black digital watches . . .

Susceptible humanity has in one young man, a poet, an invisible tyke who likes to shock through the window panes of his fog... through his still, murky mind.

Wobbly, topsy-turvy energy . . .

. . . A grossly insatiable perversion of human mores—like looking up a little girl's skirt at an adult function . . .
A holy rapist, dribbling jeweled saliva, turning on all the womenfolk. And then, in us: the hot demon that knows, caged in every human temple, looking out through icy, cruel eyes that are like little television screens of falling static . . .

And behind religious walls: A deified, golden cobra, guarding an empty pool; the serpentine headpiece of
. . . a long forgotten, freshly horrendous face, staring at you through the plane of this "swimming pool" that magnifies the hot bed of a strange presence . . .

This face, resting timelessly in the stars of its spiritual deserts and galaxies. The gods need peace too . . .

As do humans, whose

urban antennas send out

shimmering waves
in day-light beauty, the waves—far flitted through to
blood skies over merchants and modern northern cities—
another chapter in god's book of solitude and creeping stealth.

Wily worms and snakes . . . waves

Sweet, cosmic impulsions
          broadcast into the blue and beyond;
                    resacralized spermatozoids,

following home

          through the cold night sky . . .

Droided heroines of night,

like a child's glazed vision of wet car lights in sacred traffic . . .

Scarred forever by this lingering memory that glides through
snowcapped mountains

and most sterile of days. Little shadow . . .

The spermatozoids—

The prayers of everyone's quickened thoughts . . .

          Stories coming our way, minutely, like drizzle . . .

          The east's story hovers near . . .

You can feel the glare of the Gods,

                    their energy . . .

. . . We're little pools of water at the roots of unfathomable
mammoth trees . . .

. . . How can brine fathom itself, let alone the whale?

Or so they say.

As a song has as its title:

"Feel the universe"

Its unbearable beating, its deaf pounding of excitement in the shallow, craggy shores of your soul's pleasure and the cavity of your body . . .

Feel this tracing line through the decades . . .

Surreptitious staring—it's all not even there when you look away . . .

Where do we go?

Fugue men and women start new lives in deserts with Bedouins after the death of their western lovers—fallen to pieces like red or white rose petals . . .

Sometimes, you can feel the fever pitch of sultry conniving in the conspiratorial air of our western machinery of living . . .

"Ride the king's highway . . . "

In the bustling,
winding streets of Kathmandu
flaring away . . .

And the slaked mountains . . .

Full of marijuana, packed with lassies and maritime cops . . .

The eastern minds: thick as a thousand Ganges . . .

. . . as trillions of memories . . .

. . . The earthly ones softly glimmer in the

rainbow days where they met their closure . . .

Fold the worlds away . . . Fold them away in play!

American Dream

America, flow beyond permutations and micro patriotisms
and diversions of secret life and strangeness of times, in this
soft expansiveness of country, exploding softly, softly erupting
mother nation. Shelter me in these downtown malls.
Let me sink into her lap. And ask her if I can stay there
for a while in tender and white-thin orbit.
I am this shining satellite—shut out by doors
of diffidence and silence. Still, there is some way that's finer . . .
Some truth hangs, still, like a vein of river of promise.
Contact and hail the Lords. Pour ashes into the sky,
billowing our dreams and desires . . .
I am this vein of pulsing euphoria in a pretty woman's oval nail
like the glass-smooth, soft pink patch in her bathroom,
radiating sensually: soft overdrives, redundant miracles.
Today's wise gold heroes are driven away from here;
only the truly miniature stay behind in this land.
Let's leave them be. Let's live in the clouds like
those men, next door, on leashes with their strange laments;
in the cryptic vault of night. What's more:
grant me the tanks of aroma of awesome estate . . .

Champion bodybuilders are melting,
in '70s color TV, into your living rooms . . .

You found yourself locked out of your apartment.

At last, safe from where the fast streets murmured
and flew the banners of your rape

Sitting back to wall outside of apartment, you
took a sodden tennis shoe off.

Instead of a foot, a lit-up and colored forked tongue . . .

Same with other foot!

I am the satellites' mercurial rivers
and the rivers' tributaries of primal knowing,
like the lit-up, forked tongues.

What a wild taste!

Like the first time they showed you a Muppet's foot—
running away—on TV.

My America

Shoot Whitman, rocketing through my veins,
gushing sweet waters of comets and stars,
wet sheets stretched over God's eyes.
Gush commas and blue sunsets and giraffes
and circle-shaped skies—where dirt-skinned vagrants go to fly.

America is in June's shimmering fair hair,
black and unbraided, her creased smiles
rippled away, her naturally uncompromising ways
and portals to dark peace. Portals to lavish oceans
whispering at palace doorways . . . Godless revenge
swimming up through the hills, through your earphones . . .
Lithe thinker in divine tank of diving, opening my device . . .
Such an unhippie from the land of Saint Francis . . .
I pursue her golden galleries, her ghastly dresses . . .

I am this boy in America, to whom what can mean
finery or impressions like sensual-jeweled
gold mugs with lathered foam
in bars—dissolute and manly.
A boy, lost his mother to the Andes from the Alps . . .
The heavy tongue of air holds her peace . . .
This tracking love and search of a boy.
How is this small reality of sorrow?
Pens wonder and falter. Words and pages
fall asunder, suctioned into white quicksand.
They fall apart like worlds bursting at the seams with world
wars.

Anduquis is in my heart and in my ear, this violet lush of a flower rushing
near my heart, in a vein coasting Africa, and far out countries in the sky . . .

I am the American sun, the early morning sun—trilling, stretching in through your windows . . .

I am sunshine and love of big days and lavender and peach, overly scented blankets and things in mall stores, with this legally narcotic haze.

And I am palace-bright kitchens and home-style casseroles—funds of tar and sun and plastic melting and bridges and a hypnotic soldier-emission in the crystal day. I am all these, but the mothers paved with mint . . .

———

Dense American neighborhood, immigrant youths: Wondy, Rayna, and Chie are up early in high rise. They're devilishly, manically, urbanly dancing. From them comes a screech of energy-ecstatic scream of shock and release at my naked Christ body in the street, in the blue morning . . .

And I walked up to the children of the street, the immigrant children—hearing their thoughts. Their minds spoke; they needed jackets. They got thrown out in the street without a key

. . . in the morning of this American underground . . .

With hovering, faded devils, prophets . . . The summer has come . . . I'm getting away from the sleazy man; I'm taking away my sensuous child body . . .

I am baby blue summer picnics bursting, burning in the outer fringe of Spirit's and Lore's ether, persisting in a world's secret canon of beautiful fascination, smoldering . . .
A girl and boy together eat a strawberry at once,
pointing towards some northern garden and endemic paradise

where I see nightingales, wrapped in glow of silver light,
pouring forth from boys; they're belonging to house with little leaving,
quashing children by syrupy Rolls-Royces . . .
I am impossible charisma and the spirit of love,
of yellow mammoth butterflies—lilting,
and curdling pink creatures—exuding love . . .
I am this American seed,
bred of cool, born in dark house—
isolated in dreams.

Superlove—cream of the Easter sky.
I remember the ghost of breath of the false, soft wings of American childhood
and this sublimest, lightest beige God and crystalline, crying Cinderella.
The drives and paper rabbit ears in evening—with its clamorous moons . . .
I am lemonade stands and magic markers and cotton candy,
the weak smiles of brown faces prospering in the heat,
toiling in little ways like creaking ice-cream cone makers, faces
with glistening humility in naive and nice tenderness of
exchange; I am skyscrapers.
Rumbling prisons in the night,
dogs baying in the peak of the world,
slanted rain hitting our Hollywood.
I am the roaring timberland youths assembled in street
corners with a visage and no discernible
cause or destruction planned,
like a broad, chestnut beauty's legs—
wide open, lithe and tangled as thunder, harmless and limitless;
terrifying and jocular—like mountain ranges, engulfing silly
little men, the mountains' pores pouring over with supercilious
sounds of reason and senses of sex.
And a porous land of wise, young libertines,
where a sheltered boy sheds most of his fear of moving about
with drugs. Where every day is God and he makes love
to a blond thing under the stars.
"You took me in, my friend."
I am cities dotted with peopled wildernesses

shunning us out like suns behind bars,
walking down big city blocks with single tear frozen in its
track, half-way down face—
the northern inhibited star of misery.
Miserable memory chides my bored, drooling boots
of homeless drones and trolls. The soft, thick bell tolls
for some—those of longevity in waxing and waning.
Surprise them with the golden treasure chest of killers.
I am doctors' visits doused with Christ.
Enter our strange dream of generium;
slipped off like those vile, dusky shoes.
The visits—Devil encased by fast evening.
I am the founting glory of peace in parks with baby deer.
This light rain falling of asylum and the leprous spirit of music.
"Call out to her . . . "
I am a young woman named Liberty, deprived of
delight, sealed into unfeeling envelope,
at the mercy of God's unprying fingers,
laughed at by high-energy comics,
blessed by races and their infinitesimal spewing peoples
under the braiding, diamond sun,
forfeited under father's smile, at the edge of this existence . . .
I am the integers of invading memory
and unquiet of egotisms
quelled by their very own drink, silver and platonic.
I'm going with the girls to the unnerved lake, unromping,
to unearth my oldness. Stoned driver, captain youth;
slouch-backed flyer; beaten down by life's, by kingdom's
multitudinous waves . . .
I am alone walking through an evacuated city
with face of burning Moses and artery of celestial sky,
contacting empty basin of swimming pool
Electric mammoth snake sleeps like Herod, maintaining
equilibrium in dark lakes; this sundry division in your psyche;
Sunday will come wily some day and you'll see or sleep
forever, careless, dressed in lace . . .
The boy strides forward with Herod's pulse,
with the peculiar wish of a boy dreaming in his soft, petaled
mind, softly dawning embarrassment of sun
Pitiful creature of obsession—lend him a license, a black line;

cover him in night's ultraviolet swan.
He says: unlock me from death's silence.
I wish to enter, to drizzle myself in so many golden
Cleopatras and spearmint, neon nights (pulsing in safety of
wildernesses
of sweet glory).
Roman girl . . . Aqueduct . . .
Her prettiness trickles like my thought.
The black ink of night-beauty in a river down my shoulder
blade, like encased laughter set free and washing up on a shore,
fragrant girl-hair, combing soft hysterias in the heart.
Colombian, Bolivian girl—heresy . . .
You know: I am unchecked spiritual power and effulgence.
I am the loving and their kindred and the unloved.
Come hidden love, brake with the sound of the trees;
wish them into larger and kinder life . . .
I am light postures beckoned by the drooling sun of a lithe
kingdom. . .
I am the lies of mysticism: lame, hunched over
characters, drowning beside their beige-grey syrup on the
sidewalk.
And I am the truths of all men. And, maybe even,
I am workshops of glory in the twilight of an age . . .

Silence and Contact in the American Day . . .

Dying diamond necks and swan girls—humble, munificent—
met in embracing love of soft colors at city corners
breathed into our ether and secret history.
I have the phantom of this memory . . .

Girls—thinking divine softness, out of sync with major mania
of grown-ups' ashy, marbled metropolises and their impervious
summons. The girls are disrupted gratefully by the sweet
thought-telethons of a candied male youth. We televise our
faces; I'm sending out these pulsing waves of sweet prayer of
sediment of heart. Wax, girl, on the outer glisten of my eye; I'll
let you into its dark neverlands of delicious. It's really sweet and
personal—this contact with ageless girls. Softly, subtly dying to

the waves of technology, I sometimes think . . .

When alone and, especially, when on grass,
I am this wise, delicate infant master
like a daisy staving off suicide—living, breathing on edge of chair . . .
I am an hourglass youth, melded into your next-door neighbor.
Displaced and thin waste, thin wave-man, like drops fallen in water
into Asian American paradises of stillness . . .

Time whistles, abruptly thrusting her face through tiers of
white clouds, soaked in heresy . . .

Wait for a fragment; for a second;
time loans me its smile; Caldas whispers
white beauty, yearning neighborhoods and
whispery sliver. Flash the microscopic view
of the ships and the prayer of a girl smile.
Put dreams to bed to refresh the lanes of your memory
and forever endless youth. She beckons without motion
and without tiring from afar—this is one whisper: "mayday "
So soft . . . this quivering tyranny of girl
and clime . . .

The whisper subsides . . .

He listens to hear the sexy,
greenish stars shivering from a
dark universe thriving hard . . .

The people pass by
in his infinite losing streak . . .
He looks on at them as they go by . . .
Smack mankind in the face with a bright green hammer. A soft one . . .

The American Night. Its Theatre and Spilling Secrets

He's enclosed in the prison of his angel's suspension of breath,
in their light gold-braided tears, when night becomes
heroic and soft . . .

You'd see him walking and running transversally . . . in the
night . . .
where this sound may be found
racing in comet-stream along dusty, smutty roads of South
American city . . .
inebriated spirit of ray
partial prayer
Desire
Racing code; peculiarly lucid
splendidly released beneath
The ray dives succinctly through the city's atmosphere . . .
It is one more masked heroine, granted to night as herald of
west;
just noticed by nightfall's festival
. . . falling . . . into
. . . her champion neighborhoods . . .

Engross me in motley, Asiatic neighborhoods of scent-rivers of secret sense. Carlo in the ghetto blaster coursing with his play through my veins and nerves like grass and unpopulated mind-fields of dreams . . . Play the music of the grass . . . There were the ways to school and the melting asphalt of June. "See you soon." In the umbilicus of heavy summer, in its day was stirring water on the curbs, our eyes dribbled and distilled this quiet American God, instilled in the black breath of speakers and the heaving, breathing walls, still unknown. Parceled feeling—chartered away, slammer of chest. Our minds could have flown out on the charter flights of rays into the celebrating sky—myriads into the sky's soft brains. But, then, there was almost lucid flight on a Lucy's white wings, spun from these innocent house parties, graced thick with raw girl beauty and the happy sight of night. I looked out through hungry elephant eyes and there were these lost boys. At the end of adolescence, we were this floating on fountains, getting high in bathroom stalls, playing. Since then, I have sat before ladies that are my mothers and shed violet tears. And, still, in this day, I open my arms,

awaiting the greatest and lightest gift from the black, sultry sky.
—Come, desired brother, born in June: I'm sending every last inch of myself . . .
I am selling out . . .

These neighborhoods of night . . .
. . . stealing behind
. . . the watered glow of heavy and sleeping silence . . .

What days have bestowed to the soft and delicious gallery of night's surface, betrays the girls' childish streak. Girls run from home, swallowed by the city, rushing to become unlicensed clowns, leaving seventy-mile trails . . . Damn their minds. And their cool water eyes—pouring down their licorice bodies as salving grace . . .
. . . These brushed on night—bluish ghosts—melting off . . .
They remind a person of cartoon elephant tears. Thin-leafed tears of saddened elephant, blown away;
like so thin bean slices for the gravely poor and small . . .

The disgraced, distanced girl-ghosts waver one last time and disappear into the night . . .

Breathe the night

The ray trickles silently in the night of this world . . .
and flows in the musty ways and rivers of some "ether," or some trash in the nightly and windless stillness; the ray is perceptible only to us . . . Our prayer surges, discernible only to us, lightly rustled into this enclosing life. We were life's naive captives. We thought it was poised to leave us forgotten in the well of our prime, written across our hearts and the city walls. We, at the bottom, had wished only to be, sweetly, the intelligible characters in its dream, in a great god's tablet. Bound with my brother in secret suffering and hope and almost traceless
love . . .

Or, maybe, it was just life billowing by . . .
No curses or blessings added . . .

In such a soft dream . . .

Emulsion of New Day. And Diet of Ecstasy . . .

Will I rise forever with the lethargy of spirit's dew in these precincts? And your jubilant smiles come through zooming, large and starry as April's ships. Come through: the dew's cracked-open suns, streaming light, finer; into a spotless urbanity, or into screaming flowers; they're unspeakable. My sister and I are lilies broken from the sidewalk cracks, withering baby towers. Let me be this slivery ghost soul where I'm this smoldering brown energy repairing for the emergency of night's pharmacy. A life-ecstasy wells up in my home and time. Right now! Does this bleached day ever enter our minds and nerves? It's all so simple. The beautiful girls and boys scream: "Right now!" Beat these suns like egg yolks into a new and blown-up life of fruity, goddess-dames shaded in downtown malls, coming down over me with their dream-laden hair. And city christenings that render me nice in the city's mature machine and apparatus of night.

I am the rivers of essence coursing through a city. I am the cool shadow that rises at dawn like the backwaters of your dreams. I am going to feel this bright new world of me and all—with strength—in my fibers . . . And to repair for the night . . . in relief . . .

And what of chaos urbanity? What of soft, poetic violences—the city's demented daylight melodies and nature. Thrust forth these inordinate beauties and digital songs. Go forth silly police who weigh not even an ounce—falling below the hill—never catching up . . .

Give me this place in society's sun, amid the best of urban slickness, with the savors and scents of a hovering paradise . . .

To well up on a foreign shore to the sunshine of every day . . . this surreal and
stupendous American youth. This radiant youth . . . This musical
youth . . .

Little Sciences . . .

A human is drawn to the lowest frequency.

Spit at youth. Give a hail and salute to some emblem of universal hate. Pluck the chords of her soul and make high music of her sensual landscape and touching earth with soft fire and naiveté, leaving craters in the earth . . . Where this woman's body reminisces in the aggressive sun rays . . .

An emergency trickles down into a mild sound from out of town that moves and booms like a river. Like a fine behavior

Palm tree twins shed over sparkled sand, scattered across nightness . . . There's a zooted cool loner with the wet cosmos starring in his camel eye . . .

Drizzly dancers occupy the night, drizzling over self. Where commercial beauties aren't appealed to—that Latin, arabesque, or, somehow unnamable, scent of small nectarous blossom, fills the
air . . .

Today. Our Future . . .

Meandering miles wide, I'll bury my foil in this earth.
While you all pick up the tears of my demise . . .
Your cataclysmic laser day of sun echoes out like vatic shrieks
of night vultures. I am the small driver in the zenith . . .
Rembrandt hinges from a voice in another room
or from a possessed finger.

Humanity is losing the race against its dreams . . .

My brain smiles in its theatrical cloud of despair.
I am the pulsing of every pill of a space shuttle,
racing into the darkened skies . . .
Leaf through the pages
of the pale-colored

chamber-magazines,
soaked in dense heresy
and mystery—
of this place—the earth . . .

I wish poetry for the pink
and chrysalis-soft soldier in my iris's
doorway—he means to communicate
with a frozen house or bleak star
(sprinkling sister)—or with a stone
lodged in the blackness of god's eye,
a stone—befallen tunnels and streams of music.
A stone—molded in the thirsty prison of a strong infant
who laid ancient claim to
splitting suns, with their near guarded gardens—
hazed spearmint places.

The prayers for my entelechy
send hairy and fragrant
words from these Edens.
Break to the world of life,
where father breathes as gold seraph,
where mother is massive bone and floods,
and a million arms rush
on in waves . . .
Virile alarm of water rushes from the arms, from the sky . . .

On a Sunday, Pacific grandfather,
let me die beside you in cat-like peace.
Turn the ground into membrane.
I have something to say to humanity
that I cannot put into words
from the abyss of my blue-tinged heart.
Nobody gives but a damn.
Everyone rests in their homeostasis and private, relevant
plights.
Spread families spread over death.
Love these lulling rivers of strong tears
at the nexus of freedom . . .

and blue lightness . . .

You know, we're treading in the sea.
We're walking beside silent tram track,
over shallow ocean, over urban city peace.
We might be hunting the wars and ghost
of pre-existence.
Come over us, wet, vainglorious dawn . . .

Desire . . .

American . . . Eternal and Becoming . . .

From dimly lit rich abode—youth's desire tears through selfish
tiers—damsel-sisters crying in veins of glory behind doors.
A curtain draws over you of white gold filaments.
Ballerinas and dancers fly out
in the storm of a Bayader through the Caspian night . . .

Here we go . . . now . . .
youth's desire comes:

. . . rugged cascade . . .

. . . fall into the ancient homeland at celebrating dusk . . .
. . .million-hand-clapping dusk . . .

. . . smithereens . . .

An insatiable count reinvents his cruelty,
become stern legend. Fixed like a skylark
in its sweet trajectory—passage of remembrance
to the strange hospitality of this dark and peculiar guest.

Or . . . the sweet, night guest in a fragrant land . . .

. . . nightingale . . .

A gold desire, weighed up against vast tons
and the cold salad of boredom and humanity;
never waned away. All these waivers
writhing in eternity's cemetery . . .

Your ancestors . . .

They are luminous angels . . .

The ant has her trove . . .

The anima its chamberous ray of rebellion,
          stricken in the heart and isle of an eye . . .

          For humans the war is on. No one runs from
the massiveness of the water;
          And there are these installments of flights, flitted out
far from the personnel of man and sempiternal secrets of
industrial espionage . . .
                    Desire sits, sinks and rivets and breathes,
as meaning's black dentures persist—the biting means of
making sense.
Ziaphonic skull of meaning . . .
          I can hear through the
dreams of your conversations . . .
                    Your conversations dream through each other

          The sky's old stars are foppish foes—better yet,
wilt-haired and shrewd gods—in so many places at once . . .
                    The foes slither and pattern in lamp post, in
fabrics of reality . . .
          These are etched lessons on the starry plane of vast
memory's mystery . . .

Unlike the lit web, where you'd dance away from the
dunderheaded freak—instead,
the vast plane's dark mountain
and darkened butterflies carved from air . . .

Dusky fruit plucked from

valley orchard
at unharming dusk,
ripened in our mouths by the evening—
these luscious baby rivers.
A god has left his knives and
satisfaction of guns behind for the toilers and renters.
And a fire burns in a peak in my eye,
"here we go, hold on . . . "
Ancient perfume,
laundromat sighting in the night,
A triple déjà vu—

home . . .

There is a gold-braided desire never lost on man,
while any spirit can remember itself, and pharaoh
has some precious wave that sends him sleepless
through the summer night.
A precious and astral dust of glitter.
A night made of moon.
Seeing and feeling God in a
shot-up stem of wheat and the quiet universe.
Or a worn and severed pharaoh's cracked
opening into oceanic sky
of dazed happiness where lingering
crickets creak to the
sky's sell-out beauty—
fed intravenously to wanters in the night,
laid down like feathers,
like flyers beneath the stars . . .
And pharaoh has relinquished
all wishes to send spheres or basins on missions into the
heavens, crouched from his bed and dearth of intrepidness.
He is happy to sit on earth.
Plastered in the roof of his hearing:
nearby tropical wildernesses.
They broadcast across
airport terminals.
Burst above: the peal of
female voice of

strange and sweet authority.
The pilots, like patients, never travel far;
thrusting not too beyond their viscous rest; dallying eternally;
they're shy, like children, to the brightness of the tropic's
sounds.

Desire, golden and hare-brained.
I can feel my spirit's coolness by the banks of night . . .

Raw youth's desire, like relentless city overpasses at night, this
tangled wonder goes out into clear skies of coolness of the
American summer . . .
It is the string that links the lengths of men's lives and the
expanses of their consciousnesses—like the gilded ocean
shores.

Desire flies out like overripe spices and fertility and nepotism, overflowing into this golden cup I hold up to a lightening blue sky, sloshing down this impossible cerulean gravy across the graves of my heart . . . This unutterable treasure in my ears . . .

I loved stoned beauties and their wet stars
in garrulous and gathering night's excitement . . .
its cryptic heavens and rooms . . .

I'll throw them all away,
if you can just whisper to me this one secret:
that I'd never to have pray to a god again . . .
and I'd run away with more than any world could contain . . .
And I would miss nothing . . .

I'd sing like a tall grass Sally. Where is this Sally?
This sundry sun; this specimen of a girl; this specimen of a
lickable interface with the centerprise of all dreams and heroes
and cool nights thrusting into nests of never . . .

There must be this Sally, soured with the stars' tears like
cherry candy strip. Vision of a natural mother
through light rain and wilted hair,

like the wheat, washed away . . .
Tell us, in plaintive whispers,
of a way to a natural and hypnotic compassion
that radiates our bodies away . . .
Our "holy," our "wholly"
of a digital sun that would leave us dying in the woods . . .

Feminine dirty-blonde
woman enters a concert hall
with a man by her side.
Tears liltingly bouncing off
her cheeks with every little sob.
And there is this quiet blanket
of shame that covers everyone.

can you remember if you ever saw this?

Give me a chance
and
my soul
will flood the city.

Notes from the American Underground and More . . .

In the permissive sun of the American underground, I am kids on tarmacs, laid without care and custom, blowing insolent marijuana smoke streams, shocking immigrant neighbors . . .

I'm the raspy voice of this son who told me he'd been shunned by the American dream. The dream spat on his face and lodged a crystalline splinter in his soul.
The rest is backstreets and history and the sentiments of stories rippling into the heart of the world and into the narcotic night

I dazzle things and places with this blinding
light of reality, echoing the Holy Spirit,
that beauteous star shattered in the northernmost skies . . .

I saw a melodic comet—child prodigy—frozen overhaul—

streaking and screaming by overhead like an F-16 . . . Sepulcher
on parade . . . Conniving with the flash in your eye . . .
Blacking out elderlies' eyes.

In the American spirit, I am beneath and
above all things—
the last American shaman,
with blue eyes of magnetic power,
under ground, fast below a small lonesome flower that is
winking on the earth.
Shaman flies through the soft corridors of dreams . . .
Run through the lands of Jules Verne and decepticons . . .
Through tough and gentle nature's sprouting
of demure science of freak jizzly genius—
welling up from its cracks of dwelling with persistence . . .

He is the one that teaches
me every little fraction of being humility.
Come Andean, African-faced youth.
Supernatural leader of washed-out cities and brains.
Leader of wildlife and NYC . . .

The big, laned parks sleep, await . . .
Praise to these brains and torpedoes and
men and things in our gentleman's chamber of dense color,
grand mirrors and collapse of minds . . .
The house, at the zenith of the parks, is—somewhere—
singing its sweetened song with glee.
Take a magazine off the shelf. Stare into its figures and strange,
dusty, god-like maneuvers. All this weird scenery. I wonder
what it does to your soul?
I hear snakes in the wilderness. And a snake takes the sky—
wide-eyed and long; it means to rupture the entrails of your
dreams. Humanity, bound by its place, by its slouching wall of
complacence. The snake of the sky runs like water—winding
this way, like when you misplaced your phone or wallet, grave.
Our soul resounds like long hair, but that is merciful, like the
stubble of the earth and wide-mouthed lilies receiving the
vespertine sky and once beautiful and paltry promises in night.
Like the greatest gift, or highest treason. Rush to the gates . . .

Bring in the congregated diamonds and rubies of obeying youth, and beckoning daughters—run into the highways—breaking up. The soft temple of mediocrity is rising. Bring in the daisies and the love of our human value—this starry digit. Bring in the music of the satellites . . . Regal yellow . . . cold shower of morning sky . . . purple-roofed. Come sweet apocalypse . . . Your breath and bread in the sky . . . Leavens of softest, speaking desire, spiral staircases into black infinity . . . This cause of unbroken soul . . . The sky is coming down in swoon . . . The children rush from under the stairs, from tepid life of soft light . . .
Hurry on us stones of violet sky,
clean, American, spearmint faces—impressed by strange and dense-distant beauty . . .
Jump-skip ten levels on the spiritual computer game in the woods of the neighborhood . . . A chip could contain it all. Hail on me. Hail on us these stones . . . Will the water run? Run all these primalities . . .

Turn on the TV. Entire and noble states—lit up enterprise ships of godly and colored wealth and money rest upon such complacent power as this. The weight of a television wave in palm . . . Enterprises turn on man's axis of stillness and grace. But, what is this figure that hides around in subterranean continent? Waiting for his moment . . .
He is no head prophet,
no more than fumes have virtue
and shriek at praise,
vanishing into themselves.
He would have himself interred
before debuting today.
Call me: squeaky or oink
when I'm not this bulbous
musculature of the earth and this spirit . . .

Santiago's Enthralled Night Sky

The enthralled sky is in a flood of a whole nation taken up

with pots and spoons under the regime indentured with pathos
and rosy-bottomed girls in the sky,
girls trickling down to hearth of home
as licking adolescent sensuality,
its awesome, lilting music, playing coast to coast.
Beaches are bearded sunspots tentacling out to a blue sun.
The sun's fiddles collapse from its playing.
Throw out your forks and knives and all . . .
The sirens dance out alighting; they're dancers in the sky—
White shivering spermatozoids in dark, speaking silently . . .
The girls, distilled in myopic beauty like the fragment of an
atom-sun under scope, drip down in time in slutty teenage
dance halls. High in the window-specked mega-towers of
winded enterprise, the girls lick down like knives of prettiness.
Flasks full of this fervid liquid and behavior are sprinkled on by
the men and machinations of soft and cozy tyranny . . .
Men and lesbian women wear classical poets like thin watches
on wristband . . .
Boulevards become revived like beacons, like parasols and
slices of mythic strawberry shortcake—surprise in our need.

Tides of mania keep crashing on the sun of our shore.
Dampen those lights. Night embraces—guts us with its mania
into a total immersion . . .
I see lime beauties lurking in the dark like Mennonite girl eyes.
Mundane prayers and store orders are shouted from
megaphones. The fruity goddess-dames of downtown undress
in my mind under the sale's booming listings. Sale. Spring
Clearance Sale.
I'd like to steal the beauty and grace of rats—furtive creatures
like darts or arrows, hiding in bulbous, thick, shiny-leafed trees,
set off adrift in my fear/breed of imagination—spilling dark
blood varnish for this porpoise. Love the turgid scientist in his
lab . . . His house in the tree licks the hair in everyone's hearth
of daisyhood . . .
. . . I see men scaling lullabies. The ocean talks of its primal
dream—Atlantic—rapping your knuckles with wet graph paper
. . . Economists go out into the larger room—into the sweetest,
sweetest ocean . . .

Dive to the forest, to the dusk, winged dove . . .
This prayer pouring forth from my leather heart, prayer for the west. Right now I can't find much of a trace. Its scent will grow. And I wonder about pulsing doorways at night and violet airways. We were these raiders in the night . . .
Tides of mania—like a world full of me. The energy in one person to blow up the world.
Wild, smoldering, black eyes in night . . . Delicious zombies lifted from the arch-stoner's vivid, living blanket of a coffin . . .
I faintly hear a music . . .
Yes. We want something more in warmth of animals: fulcrous goodness in night. Focus on radio. We're transfixed on its sexuality—female prowess. Blow up this goodness abounding as witness to our condition.

My gentleman shaman was dining
when he was compromised in the sea of those rocking lacteal broomsticks. They said: "This is finished. It's the end."
Somewhere on a diving board: Wily, willing to dive into a pool of bones,
of suffocating crucifixes. This Gregorian champion of intactness;
of silence; of silence like prisons; of silence like silence; of silence like something . . .

Breast-fed and curled like a possum. Or was it me? On the brink of such an end;
where strange television movies stretch out into strange landscapes and intercepting highways that stand for truth . . .
and never . . .

I am this friend's highway hitchhiker. Ravenous and ready for horrorscapes
and their tiny Haitian knowledge. Come into focus, drive into heaven!

What is left, but starved ravens loitering in stark fields and the glue of
television images that won't stick?

Skip to the future: fast forward the images . . .

I remember hazed green nights in lands
and meetings with strange women . . .

I remember, in a dream, water springing up from under the
heels of me and
my cousin—so happy—as we walked down a summer walkway

And soft marches in my infant's ear—
of little military juntas
          and their relentless and soft tirading . . .

And the snow of chaos,
cloistering a
nice mind . . .
in the West . . .

I remember holding an ear up to life's lips
          and hearing such soft and dizzy music . . .
Following through the thread of a beautiful promise
to its end, we're there somehow; we're woven into this vacuum.
Come around children, 'round my garden . . .
I want to whisper at the candle flame of your hearts and
delicate minds,
and wish into your porcelain features,
and the dark peace of your God-molded eyes.
I want to hear the words spoken of my kiss with something—
unveiled like a vaudeville's forbidden theatre—forbidden
until this eternally pulsing, ringing moment . . .
He spoke the word, "nevermore," and my soul grew icy;
but I was without suffering . . .

It must be this very last frontier
at our mind's forfeiting . . .
This future promise that lingered
like an acrid smoke curl
in our college minds on grim winter days.
This archaic marriage to the

sweet and black unknown—calling like
Psalms of silence from yonder,
from dangers and summers,
from so many aliens and
galaxies and worlds—
so far away . . .
only one quantum away . . .

Fire

Beatrice rises from my belly with the fire of love, with the fire of
Blossoms—parading in silky pagan dreams of sexiest, wispiest lust and love, left closely in time. I'm left to pander with them like a starry-eyed, black-haired boy bent on loving his kindred—and on fighting with shelves,
for drinks to give to the American boys on the front curb after the dirty bike war.
Sweat-rimmed, black-haired heads—sweet . . . and falling, crashing planes.
To these do I give my due, my last heave and exhale—the last touch in me.
For these do the letters of my soul weep with tears of tender joy; of these do I speak and tell and pray . . .

Farewell . . .

Notes

Some of the poems have appeared in the following publications:

"Rain," in *Pennine Ink*, January 2012
"Sarah," in *The Sheltered Poet,* April 30, 2011
"Youth," in *A Long Story Short,* January 2012
"A Face," in *A Long Story Short,* August 2011
"The Ancient Night," in *Stepping Stones Magazine: ALMIA,* January 22, 2012
"Radiation," in *Stepping Stones Magazine: ALMIA,* February 22, 2012

Drawings on pages 25 and 34 are by Nassim Pezeshkzad; those on pages 9, 13, 40, 49, 59, and 66 are by Mathew Cullen; and those on pages 3, 21, 45, and 74 are by Benjamin Bill Cheshire.

The phrase "meiday meiday" is from the song "Canbe Atomico" by Aterciopelados.

In "Afghan Woman," the phrase "weird scenes inside the gold mine" is taken from lyrics to "The End," by The Doors.

The word "bemushroomed" appeared in *The Archaic Revival,* by the late Terence McKenna.

The phrase "Directo a tu cerebro" is from the song "Pumping Frogs" by Luke Barton.

The idea of the poem "If" was loosely inspired by "These Heroics," by Leonard Cohen.

In "American Dream," I refer to Terence McKenna's idea about a hyper dimension existing "one quanta away."

Also in "American Dream," I use my cousin's nickname, "Anduquis."

In "Archway," I invoke Jim Morrison's image "dawn's

highway," from the song of the same name. And in the poem "Kathmandu Chain" I insert the line "Ride the king's highway" from the song "The End," by The Doors.

In "Little Poet," I refer to Pushkin's famous fable, "The Queen of Spades."

In "Kathmandu Chain," I refer to the title of the song "Feel the Universe," by Juno Reactor.

In "Cursed Shore of Star," I borrowed Jim Morrison's poetic image, "soft parade," from The Doors' album of the same name.

Also in "Cursed Shore of Star," the image of Napoleon and the world was inspired by an interview with Jim Morrison, in which he described a painting he had seen in a hotel. See "Rare interview with Jim Morrison," at http://www.youtube.com/watch?v=swxMeuVQ0xk

In "Kathmandu Chain," the concept of the "hot demon" was partly taken from a metaphor in Tom Wolfe's *The Electric Kool-Aid Acid Test*, in which God is the red-hot devil inside every one of us.

In composing "Stray Sister," I apparently used a simile similar to one Lorca also used, in his poem from December 1918, "Cancion Menor," in which he compared "suns" to "spiders."

Acknowledgments

Thank you to my stepgrandfather Steve Pulley for his invaluable time and work in helping to make every poem in this collection succinct and clear in its message. Thank you to my parents for their unconditional support and love. Thank you to my sister for her lucid and sensitive grasp of fine art; she understands and affirms my role as a poet. Thank you to the three great illustrators who, through their skill and creative vision, embellished this collection of poems with wonderful drawings: Mathew Cullen, Nassim Pezeshkzad, and Benjamin Bill Cheshire. The cover illustration is "The Soul of the Rose," 1908, an oil painting by John William Waterhouse (1849–1917), provided courtesy of Julian Hartnoll/The Bridgeman Art Library. Thank you as well to Mary Anne Carswell for her assistance in putting this book together in its final form.

About the Author

Sebastian Lopez lives in Washington, DC. He is a freelance poet, spoken word artist, emcee, musician, and philosopher. Although he specialized in Russian literature at Cornell University, he loves writings from diverse epochs and parts of the world. Poets such as Vladimir Mayakovsky, Leonard Cohen, Federico Garcia Lorca, Jim Morrison, and Walt Whitman have contributed to his inspiration. He loves classical art, but has a particular passion for the power and beauty of abstract expression.

17345501R00061

Made in the USA
Charleston, SC
07 February 2013